To: _____

From: _____

© 2008 Jim Rohn International

Published by SUCCESS Books, an imprint of SUCCESS Media.

SUCCESS | BOOKS

200 Swisher Road
Lake Dallas, Texas 75065
U.S.A.
Toll Free: 866-SUCCESS (782-2377)
www.SUCCESS.com

SUCCESS and *SUCCESS* Magazine are trademarks of R & L Publishing, Ltd.
SUCCESS Books is a trademark of R & L Publishing, Ltd., dba SUCCESS Media.

Printed in the United States of America

Designed by Amy McMurry, Kim Baker and Virginia Owen

Cover designed by Kim Baker & Erica Jennings

Creative direction by Carl Waters

Edited by J.M. Emmert

ISBN-13: 978-0-9790341-3-8

ISBN-10: 0-9790341-3-2

LESSONS ON Life

HOW TO LIVE A SUCCESSFUL LIFE

by Jim Rohn

SUCCESS | BOOKS

Contents

1 Introduction

5 Fundamentals

13 Wealth

21 Happiness

29 Discipline

37 Success

45 Goals

53 Knowledge

61 Change

69 Time

77 Finances

85 Influence of Others

93 Living Well

101 Life Is Worthwhile

117 About Jim Rohn

Introduction

If we are fortunate, we one day find that person who impacts our world in such a way that our life is never the same again. By chance or by design, we meet that someone who offers the support, encouragement, and inspiration to become more than we ever thought possible.

For me, that person was J. Earl Shoaff.

The day that I met Mr. Shoaff was the day that turned my life around. This kind and generous man spent countless hours teaching me the fundamentals for successful living.

I learned much about the world from Mr. Shoaff. I hope these lessons on life that I impart to you will help bring you happiness, wealth, and success.

—Jim Rohn

Fundamentals

There are always a half-dozen things that make 80 percent of the difference. *A half-dozen things.*

Whether we are working to improve our health, wealth, personal achievement, or professional enterprise, the difference between triumphant success or bitter failure lies in the degree of our commitment to seek out, study, and apply those half-dozen things.

Success is neither magical nor mysterious. Success is the natural consequence of consistently applying the fundamentals.

Some things you have to do every day. Eating seven apples on Saturday night instead of one a day just isn't going to get the job done.

Wealth

I had always mistakenly believed that if I had more money, I would have a better plan for creating wealth. The truth is that if I had a better plan, I would have more money.

You see, it's not the *amount* that counts; it's the *plan* that counts. It's not how *much* you allocate but *how* you allocate it.

The philosophy of the rich versus the poor is:

The rich invest their money and spend what is left;

The poor spend their money and invest what is left.

Financial independence is the ability to live from the income of your own personal resources.

Happiness

Happiness is both the joy of discovery and the joy of knowing. It's the joy that comes to those who painstakingly design their lives and then live them with artistry.

Happiness is both giving and receiving, reaping and bestowing. It comes to those who deliberately expand their horizons and experiences. It resides in the houses of those who have the ability to handle disappointment without losing their sense of well-being.

It is activity with purpose. It's love in practice. It's both a grasp of the obvious and an awe of the mysterious.

Happiness is not an accident.
Nor is it something you wish for.
Happiness is something you design.

Happiness is the art of learning how to get joy from your substance.

Discipline

The most critical ingredient for success is discipline. It is the bridge between thought and accomplishment…the glue that binds inspiration to achievement…the magic that turns financial necessity into the creation of an inspired work of art.

Discipline is the master key that unlocks the door to wealth and happiness, culture and sophistication, high self-esteem and high accomplishment, and the accompanying feelings of pride, satisfaction, and success. Discipline will do much for you. More importantly, though, is what it will do to you. It will make you feel terrific about yourself.

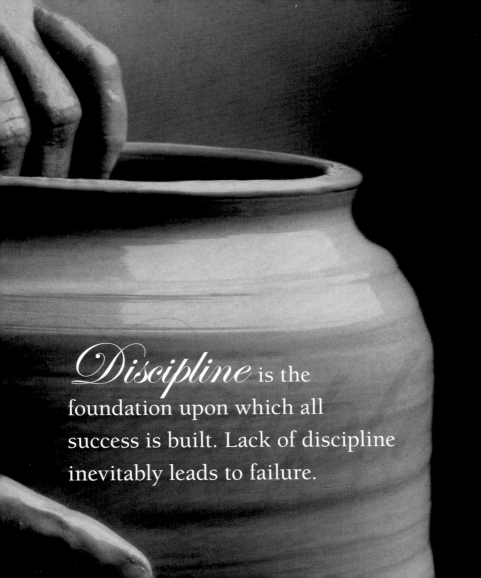

Discipline is the foundation upon which all success is built. Lack of discipline inevitably leads to failure.

We must all suffer from one of two pains: the pain of discipline or the pain of regret. The difference is discipline weighs ounces while regret weighs tons.

Success

Success is responding to an invitation
to change, to grow, to develop, and to become—
an invitation to move up to a better place
to gain a better vantage point.

Make your life what you want it to be for you—
that is true success.

Success is not to be pursued;
it is to be attracted by the person
you become.

Success is the process of turning away *from* something to turn *toward* something better.

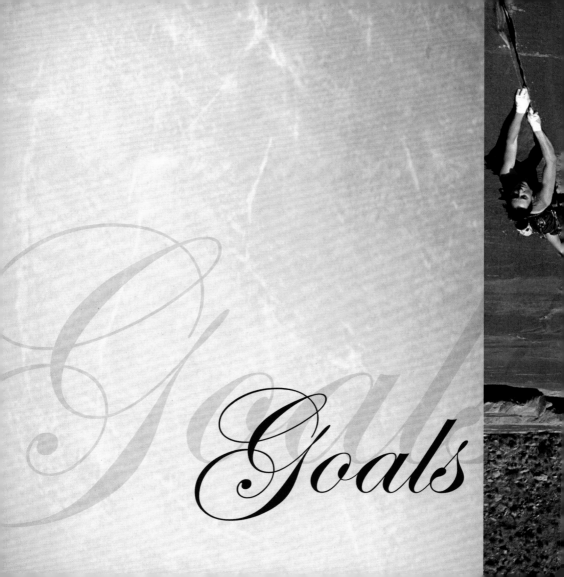

Goals

Two weeks after I started working for him, Mr. Shoaff asked to see my list of goals. I replied that I did not have any. Mr. Shoaff sighed. "If you don't have a list of your goals, I can guess your bank account within a few hundred dollars." He guessed right. And that really got my attention.

That day I became a student of the art and science of goal-setting.

Goals. There's no telling what you can do when you get inspired by them. There's no telling what you can do when you believe in them. And there's no telling what will happen when you act upon them.

Like a well-defined dream, well-defined goals work like magnets. They pull you in their direction. The better you define them, the better you describe them, the harder you work on achieving them, the stronger they pull.

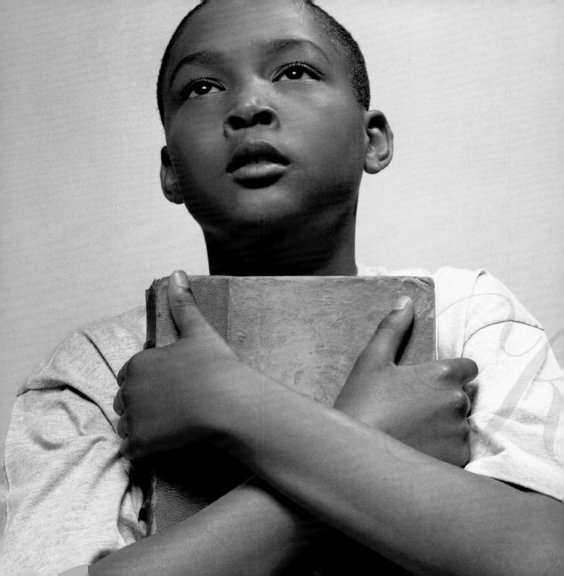

$\mathcal{O}ne$ of the fundamental strategies of living the good life is knowing what information you need to achieve your aims. I have always been a believer in the value of study.

If you want to be successful, study success. If you want to be happy, study happiness. If you want to make more money, study the acquisition of wealth. Those who achieve these things don't do it by accident. It's a matter of studying first and practicing second.

Everything you need for your better future and success has already been written. And guess what? It's all available.

Learning is the beginning of wealth. Learning is the beginning of health. Learning is the beginning of spirituality. Learning is where the miracle process all begins.

Change

Learn to work harder on yourself than you do on your job.

I've worked hard on my personal development, and I must admit that this has been the most challenging assignment of all. This business of personal development lasts a lifetime. But here's the great axiom of life: To have more than you've got, become more than you are. Unless you change how you are, you'll always have what you've got.

You can change all things for the better when you change yourself for the better.

You cannot change your destination overnight, but you can change your direction overnight.

Time

A well-fashioned day—with a beginning and an end, a purpose and a content, a color and a character, a feel and a texture—takes its place among the many and becomes a valuable memory and treasure.

As someone once said, "At midnight the winged messengers come and gather up all these pieces and take them off to wherever the mosaic is kept. And surely, on occasion, one messenger says to another, 'Wait 'til you see this one.'"

Days are expensive. When you
spend a day, you have one less day
to spend. Make sure you spend each
one wisely.

Learn how to separate the majors from the minors. A lot of people don't do well simply because they major in minor things.

Finances

If you don't know what a financial statement is, make it a priority to find out without further delay.

It's very important to know exactly where you are financially, without kidding yourself. Only when you know where you are can you possibly have a good plan for going forward to where you want to be.

Assume responsibility for keeping score of your financial life and you will take a major step towards being trusted with a life of abundance.

We all know a variety of ways to make a living. What's even more fascinating is figuring out ways to make a fortune.

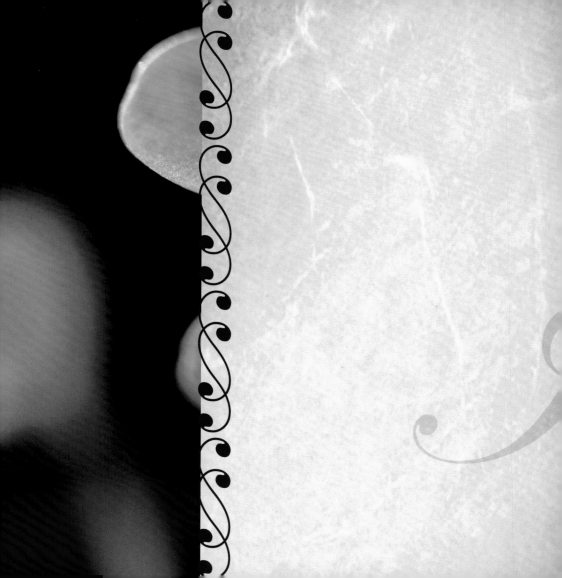

Influence of
Others

Have you ever thought about how others shape your life? Never underestimate the power of influence.

The influence of those around us is so powerful, so subtle, and so gradual that often we don't even realize how it can affect us.

Keep the weeds of negative influence from your life. "Farm" the seeds of constructive influence.

Don't join an easy crowd; you won't grow. Go where the expectations and the demands to perform are high.

Living Well

Don't just learn how to earn, learn how to live!

Some people have beautiful things surrounding them, yet feel little happiness. Others have hoarded huge sums of money, yet are poor in spirit and find little joy in their lives.

Learn the art of designing a lifestyle, the art of learning how to live.

Be happy with what you have while pursuing what you want.

The key to happiness is not more.

The good life is not an amount;
it's an attitude, an act, an idea,
a discovery, a search.

Life is worthwhile if you TRY.

Try something to see if you can do it.
Try to make a difference. Try to make
some progress. Try to learn a new skill.
Try your best. Give it every effort.

Life is worthwhile if you STAY.

You have to stay from spring until harvest.
If you have signed up for the day or the
game or the project, see it through. Don't
end in the middle.

Life is worthwhile if you CARE.

If you care at all, you will get results. If you care enough, you will get incredible results.

Care enough to make a difference.
Care enough to turn somebody around.
Care enough to change.
Care enough to win.

Life is worthwhile if you PLAN.

If you don't design your own life plan, chances are you'll fall into someone else's plan.

Life is worthwhile if you GIVE.

Giving is better than receiving because giving starts the receiving process.

Life is worthwhile if you BE.

Wherever you are, be there. Develop a unique focus on the current moment.

Let others lead small lives, but not you.

Let others argue over small things,
but not you.

Let others cry over small hurts,
but not you.

Let others leave their futures
in someone else's hands,
but not you.

ABOUT JIM ROHN

Jim Rohn is a world-renowned author, philosopher, and motivational speaker whose profound messages have enriched the lives of millions worldwide and served as the foundation for many of the principles shared by today's top personal development leaders. For more than forty years, he has devoted his life to the study of human attitudes and behavior patterns associated with the creation of wealth. His philosophy for successful living demonstrates a deep understanding of the world, and offers practical and sensible techniques that are appropriate for every business and life situation.

For more information on Jim Rohn and to sign up for his FREE weekly e-zine, visit www.jimrohn.com.

SUCCESS Magazine and SUCCESS Books offer you practical advice, ideas, and tips on leadership training, goal setting, motivation and much more. To learn more or to subscribe, visit www.SUCCESS.com.